For Jeff, always—EL

For my brother Marcu, who is a professional basketball player with incredible grit, resilience, and passion for the game. Thanks for waking up in the middle of the night to watch NBA games with me!—AB

PENGUIN WORKSHOP
An imprint of Penguin Random House LLC
1745 Broadway, New York, New York 10019

First published in the United States of America by Penguin Workshop,
an imprint of Penguin Random House LLC, 2025

Visit us online at penguinrandomhouse.com.

Library of Congress Cataloging-in-Publication Data is available.

Manufactured in China

ISBN 9798217052127

10 9 8 7 6 5 4 3 2 1

HH

The text is set in Adobe Garamond Pro.
The art was created using Procreate for sketching and Adobe Photoshop for colors,
utilizing various textured digital brushes.

Design by Taylor Abatiell

The authorized representative in the EU for product safety and compliance is Penguin Random House Ireland, Morrison Chambers, 32 Nassau Street, Dublin D02 YH68, Ireland, https://eu-contact.penguin.ie.

MICHAEL JORDAN

A Who Was? ILLUSTRATED BIOGRAPHY

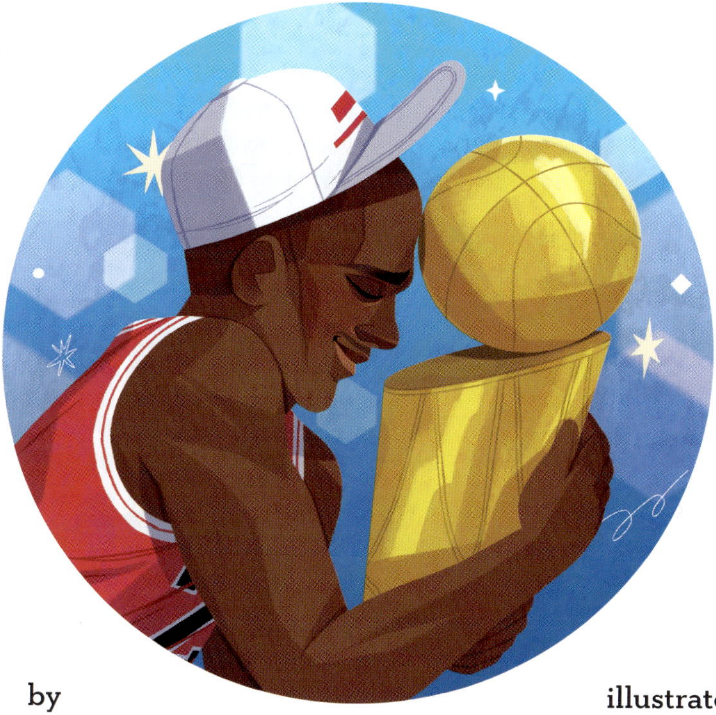

by
Ellen Labrecque

illustrated by
Alexandra Badiu

PENGUIN WORKSHOP

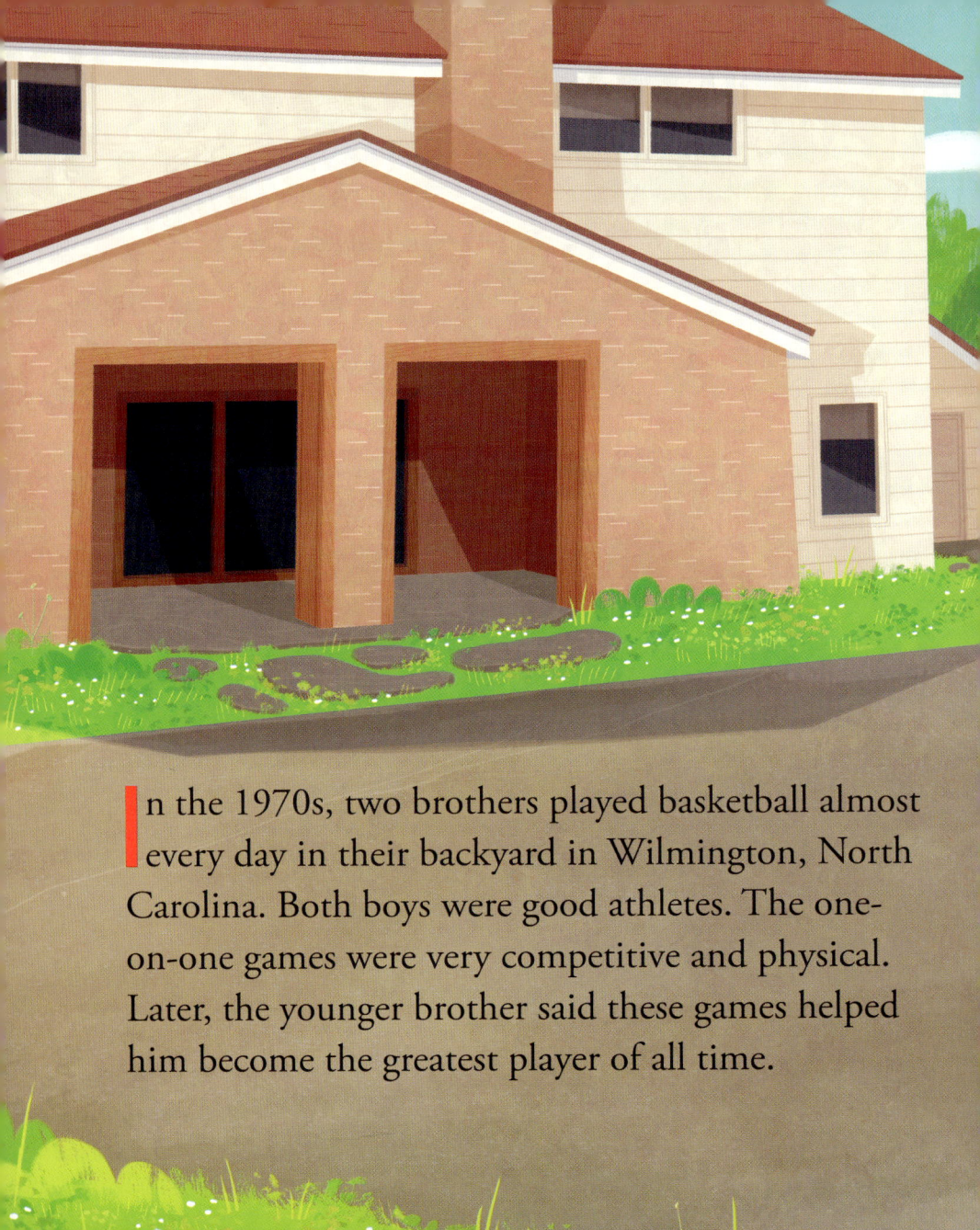

In the 1970s, two brothers played basketball almost every day in their backyard in Wilmington, North Carolina. Both boys were good athletes. The one-on-one games were very competitive and physical. Later, the younger brother said these games helped him become the greatest player of all time.

Who was this ambitious kid?

Years earlier, on February 17, 1963, Michael Jeffrey Jordan was born in Brooklyn, New York. Michael's family moved to North Carolina when he was five months old.

Michael was an active little kid. He played baseball and rode his bike around his neighborhood with friends. He thought he might be a professional baseball player when he grew up. One day, though, Michael's dad put up a basketball hoop in their backyard. It was here that Michael played with his older brother Larry.

When Michael was nine, he watched the men's gold medal basketball game between the United States and the Soviet Union in the 1972 Olympics. The United States lost by one point. After the game, Michael told his mother, "I'm going to be in the Olympics one day, and I'm going to make sure we win!"

When Michael was a tenth grader at Laney High School in North Carolina, he tried out for the boys' varsity basketball team. He wanted more than anything to make the team, but he did not. The coaches who cut him felt he was too small and thin to play on the varsity team. Michael was heartbroken and thought he might quit playing basketball altogether. Instead, Michael's mom told him to work hard and get better.

Michael began to work harder at basketball than ever before. He also got a lot taller! He grew five inches between tenth and eleventh grade. "All of a sudden you had size to go with that talent and drive," Michael's coach said. "He just blossomed."

In eleventh and twelfth grade, Michael was
the best player on the varsity team and one of the
best high school players in the whole country. As
a senior, he averaged 26.8 points per game. He
always wanted to be the best. Michael became such
a good high school player that he was one of the top
recruits in the country. Several schools wanted him
to come and play basketball for them. He chose the
University of North Carolina.

In his first season at North Carolina, Michael helped the Tar Heels make it all the way to the national championship game. In the last seconds of the final, Michael smoothly hit the game-winning jump shot! Even with the game on the line, he was not afraid of the pressure! His team beat Georgetown University, 63–62. "It was destiny," Michael said about hitting the winning shot.

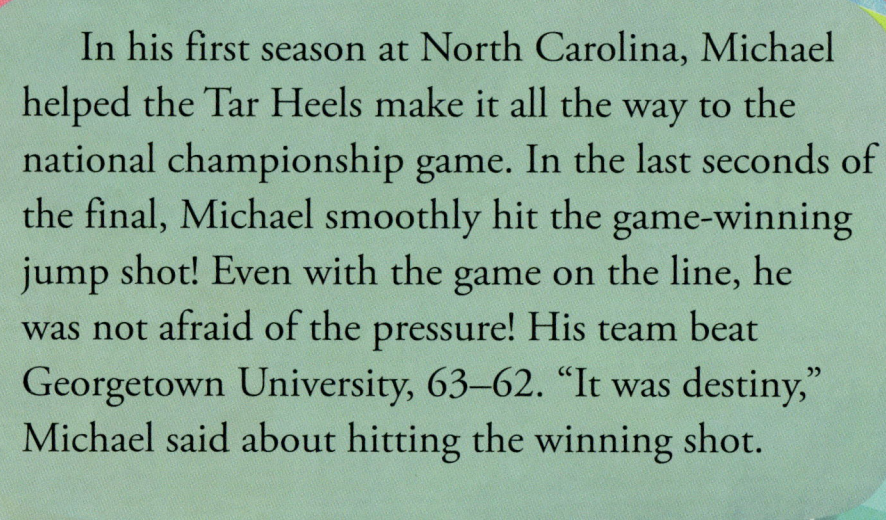

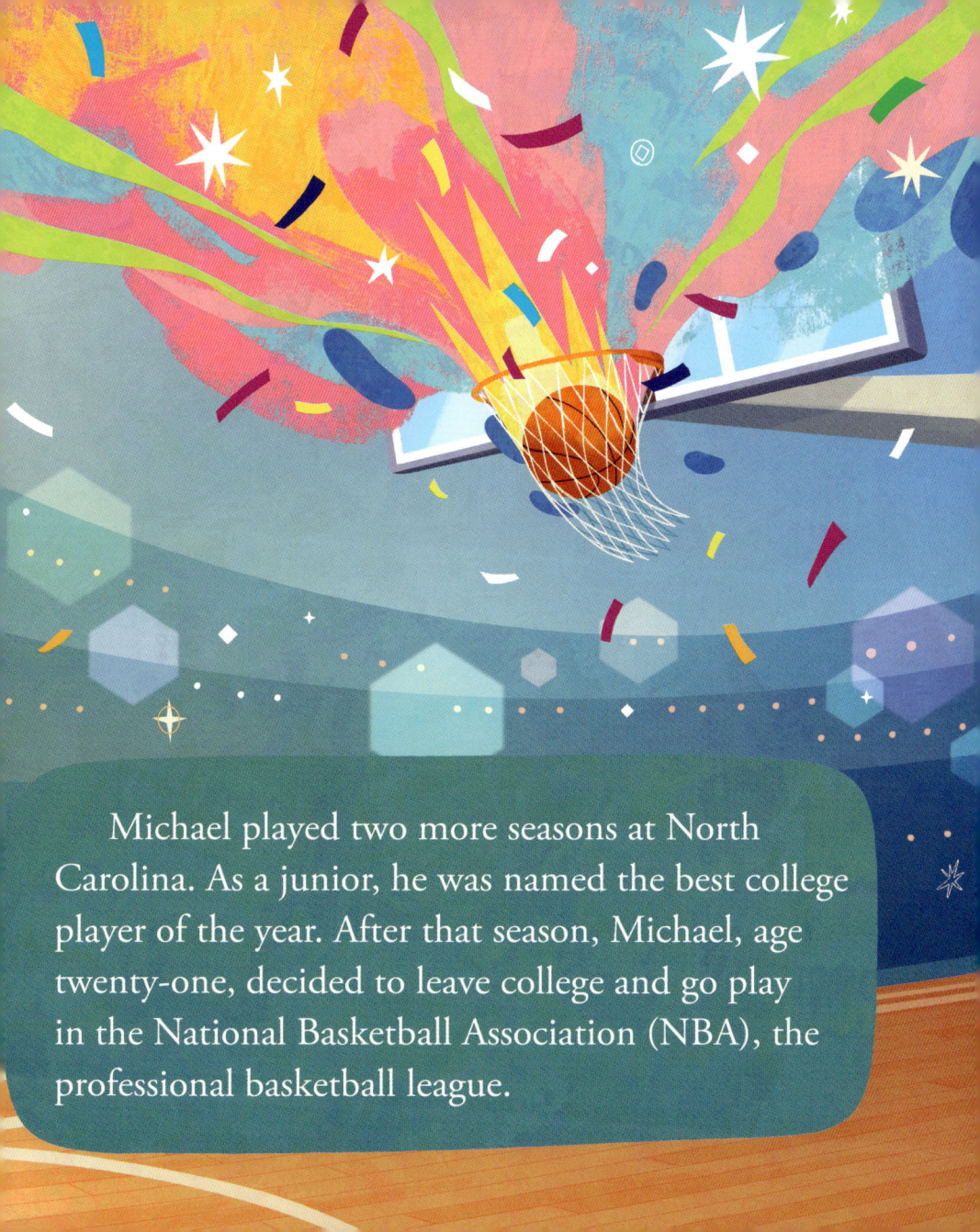

Michael played two more seasons at North Carolina. As a junior, he was named the best college player of the year. After that season, Michael, age twenty-one, decided to leave college and go play in the National Basketball Association (NBA), the professional basketball league.

Michael was one of the best players available in the 1984 NBA draft. Michael was now six feet, six inches tall, but some NBA teams wanted even taller players. The first two players selected in the draft were both over seven feet tall. Michael was selected third overall by the Chicago Bulls.

That same summer before his NBA debut, Michael played on the United States team at the Summer Olympics. The team went 8–0 and beat teams by over thirty points on average. Michael led the team in scoring, averaging over seventeen points per game. The team easily beat Spain in the final. Michael won an Olympic gold medal, just like he had told his mother he would.

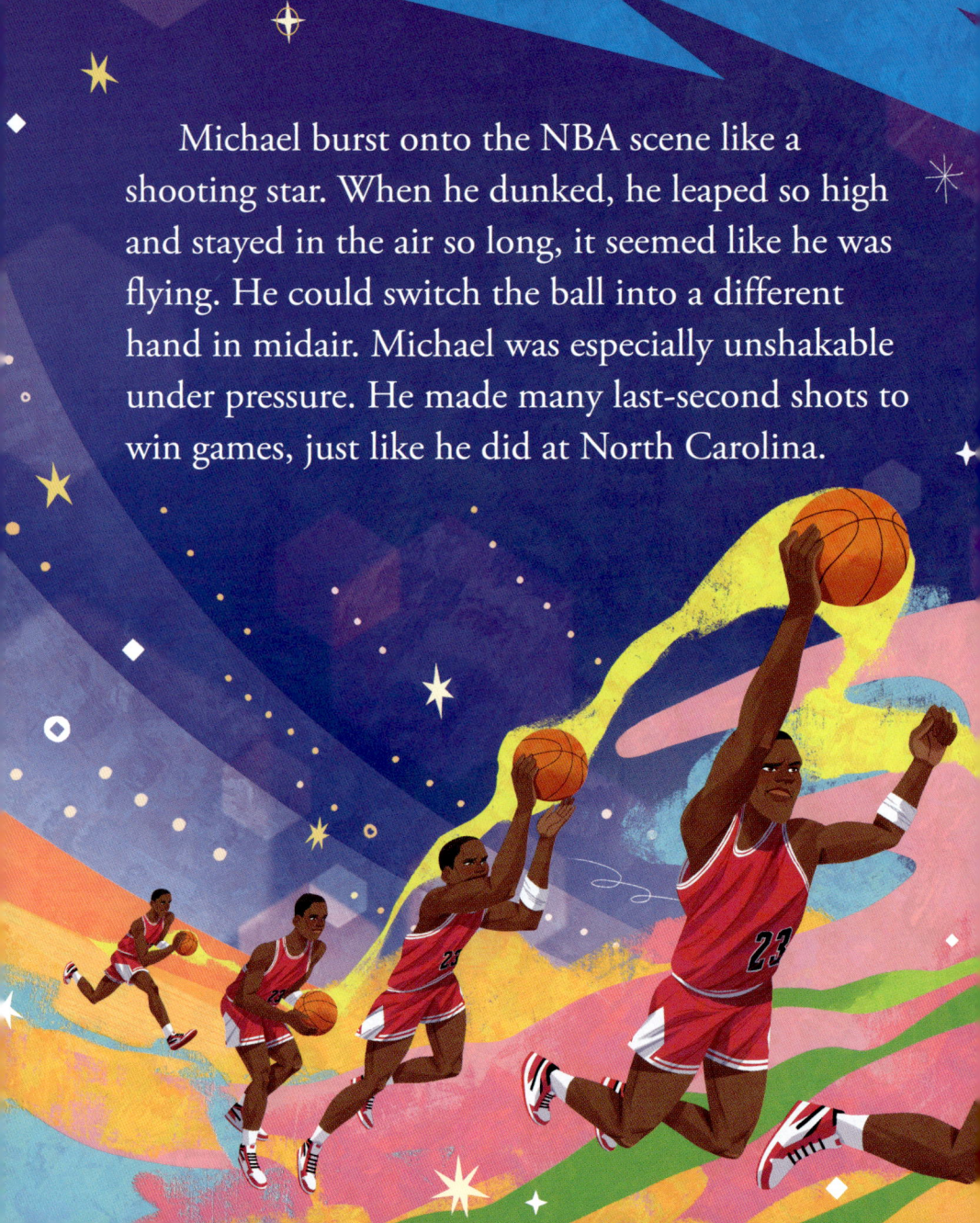

Michael burst onto the NBA scene like a shooting star. When he dunked, he leaped so high and stayed in the air so long, it seemed like he was flying. He could switch the ball into a different hand in midair. Michael was especially unshakable under pressure. He made many last-second shots to win games, just like he did at North Carolina.

Michael earned the nicknames "Air Jordan" and "His Airness." As an NBA rookie, Michael averaged 28.2 points per game and was named the NBA Rookie of the Year. The Bulls, though, lost in the first round of the playoffs. Michael was proud of all his individual honors, but he really wanted to lead his team to an NBA title.

Beginning in his third season, Michael led the
NBA in scoring for seven straight seasons. But
even as the Bulls became one of the league's best
teams, they lost in the playoffs each year. Michael
was crushed. He hated when his season ended early
and he had to watch the NBA Finals on TV like
everybody else.

Michael worked harder than ever to improve. For almost all of his career, he could always drive to the basket and make amazing dunks. But now, he became an outstanding shooter and a fierce defender. He also became a better teammate and leader.

Finally, in his seventh season in the league, 1990–1991, Michael led the Bulls to their first-ever NBA championship. Michael was named Finals Most Valuable Player (MVP). He averaged more than thirty points per game. Michael was so happy, he cried tears of joy while holding the trophy.

Michael's dominance on the court made him one of the most famous people in the entire world! His popularity helped make the NBA a hugely successful sports league.

Michael wasn't just good at basketball—he was also cool. With his 1,000-watt smile and perfect bald head, Michael starred in commercials for Nike sneakers, fast-food restaurants, and drinks like Gatorade. The Gatorade commercial made him especially famous. It featured a catchy song that said "Like Mike . . . If I could be like Mike."

AIR JORDANS

Before Michael's first NBA season, he signed a sneaker contract with Nike. This meant Nike paid Michael to wear their brand of sneakers. The deal was the biggest sneaker deal ever at the time. They named Michael's sneakers "Air Jordans." Nike releases new models of Air Jordans every year. Michael and his sneakers helped make him the biggest star in the league and, eventually, the richest. He has earned more than a billion dollars over the years from the sales of his Nike sneakers. As of 2024, there have been thirty-nine signature Air Jordan sneakers. It is the longest continuous signature sneaker line ever.

In the summer of 1992, Michael joined other NBA stars, like Magic Johnson and Larry Bird, to lead the United States Olympic team to another gold medal. It was the first time professional players were allowed to play, and the NBA players dominated.

THE DREAM TEAM

The 1992 Summer Olympics were held in Barcelona, Spain. The USA squad was nicknamed the "Dream Team" because almost every player was a legend. They won gold, scoring more than one hundred points in every game and beating opponents by more than forty points on average. The team was inducted into the Naismith Memorial Basketball Hall of Fame in 2010 and has been called "the greatest collection of basketball talent on the planet."

The Bulls won the NBA title championship again in the 1991–1992 and 1992–1993 seasons for a three-peat! Michael became the first player ever to win the NBA Finals MVP three seasons in a row! A lot of playoff games were decided in the final seconds. Michael made game-winning shots again and again. Sometimes when he scored, he had two or even three defenders guarding him!

But before the 1993–1994 season, Michael retired. In the summer of 1993, Michael's father was murdered during a robbery. Michael was devastated. He announced he would try to become a professional baseball player. His dad had taught Michael to play baseball. He wanted to honor him in this way.

Michael played minor-league baseball for one season. He was good at baseball, but he had not played since high school. He also missed basketball too much. On March 18, 1995, Michael announced to the world that he was returning to the Bulls! Once Michael came back to the NBA, he trained harder than ever. He led the Bulls to another title—his fourth—in the 1995–1996 season.

Michael and the Bulls won two more NBA titles in the 1996–1997 and 1997–1998 seasons. MJ had now won six NBA titles! Michael retired for a second time after the 1998 season. But he came back once more—this time to play for the Washington Wizards. He finally retired for good after the 2002–2003 season.

Michael was inducted into the Basketball Hall of Fame in 2009. He retired as a five-time NBA MVP, a six-time NBA champion, and a ten-time scoring champion. Another basketball great, Magic Johnson, said it best: **"There's Michael, and then there's everybody else."**

After retirement, Michael became one of the owners of an NBA team, the Charlotte Hornets. He also donated millions of dollars to charity, including $10 million to the Make-A-Wish Foundation for sick children.

Michael Jordan's name will always mean greatness. If someone refers to another person as "the Michael Jordan of" something, they mean that person is the absolute best at whatever they do. A person could be the Michael Jordan of kickball or the Michael Jordan of teaching. Michael had the heart and athleticism to be better than any other player before him—and most likely any other player after him.

BIBLIOGRAPHY

*Books for young readers

*Anderson, Kirsten. *Who Is Michael Jordan?* New York: Penguin Workshop, 2019.

Halberstam, David. *Playing for Keeps: Michael Jordan and the World He Made*. New York: Random House, 1999.

Hehir, Jason, director. *The Last Dance: A 10-Part Documentary Event*. New York: ESPN Films, 2020.

Jordan, Michael. *For the Love of the Game: My Story*. Edited by Mark Vancil. New York: Crown Publishers, 1998.

Lazenby, Roland. *Michael Jordan: The Life*. New York: Back Bay Books, 2015.

Smith, Sam. *The Jordan Rules*. New York: Pocket Books, 1992.

TIMELINE

1963 — Michael Jeffrey Jordan is born February 17, in Brooklyn, New York

1978 — Cut from the varsity team at Laney High School in North Carolina

1982 — As a freshman, makes a last-second basket to lead the University of North Carolina to a national championship title

1984 — Selected third overall by the Chicago Bulls in the NBA draft

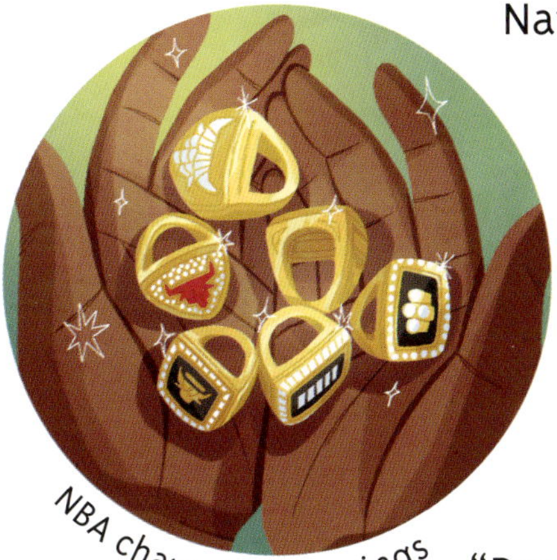

Named NBA Rookie of the Year — **1985**

Wins first of six NBA championship titles with the Chicago Bulls — **1991**

Plays on the "Dream Team" at the 1992 Summer Olympics — **1992**

Retires from the NBA for good — **2003**

Inducted into the Basketball Hall of Fame — **2009**

NBA championship rings